TROMBONE

101 MOST BEAUTIFUL SONGS

Available for
FLUTE, CLARINET, ALTO SAX, TENOR SAX, TRUMPET,
HORN, TROMBONE, VIOLIN, VIOLA, CELLO

ISBN 978-1-5400-4825-7

Visit Hal Leonard Online at
www.halleonard.com

World headquarters, contact:
Hal Leonard
7777 West Bluemound Road
Milwaukee, WI 53213
Email: info@halleonard.com

In Europe, contact:
Hal Leonard Europe Limited
1 Red Place
London, W1K 6PL
Email: info@halleonardeurope.com

In Australia, contact:
Hal Leonard Australia Pty. Ltd.
4 Lentara Court
Cheltenham, Victoria, 3192 Australia
Email: info@halleonard.com.au

CONTENTS

ALWAYS

TROMBONE

Words and Music by
IRVING BERLIN

Moderate Waltz

ALWAYS ON MY MIND

TROMBONE

Words and Music by WAYNE THOMPSON,
MARK JAMES and JOHNNY CHRISTOPHER

AND I LOVE HER

TROMBONE

Words and Music by JOHN LENNON
and PAUL McCARTNEY

AND I LOVE YOU SO

TROMBONE

Words and Music by
DON McLEAN

Moderately

AND SO IT GOES

TROMBONE

Words and Music by
BILLY JOEL

Slow Ballad, with much rubato

ANNIE'S SONG

TROMBONE

Words and Music by
JOHN DENVER

ANYWHERE IS

TROMBONE

Words and Music by ENYA,
NICKY RYAN and ROMA RYAN

BEIN' GREEN

TROMBONE

Words and Music by
JOE RAPOSO

Slowly, reflectively

BLACKBIRD

TROMBONE

Words and Music by JOHN LENNON
and PAUL McCARTNEY

Slowly and smoothly

THE BOOK OF LOVE

TROMBONE

Words and Music by
STEPHIN MERRITT

CODA

THE BOXER

TROMBONE

Words and Music by
PAUL SIMON

BRING HIM HOME

from LES MISÉRABLES

TROMBONE

Music by CLAUDE-MICHEL SCHÖNBERG
Lyrics by HERBERT KRETZMER and ALAIN BOUBLIL

BY THE TIME I GET TO PHOENIX

TROMBONE

Words and Music by
JIMMY WEBB

CANDLE IN THE WIND

TROMBONE

Words and Music by ELTON JOHN
and BERNIE TAUPIN

A CHILD IS BORN

TROMBONE

By THAD JONES

(They Long to Be)
CLOSE TO YOU

TROMBONE

Lyrics by HAL DAVID
Music by BURT BACHARACH

CITY OF STARS
from LA LA LAND

TROMBONE

Music by JUSTIN HURWITZ
Lyrics by BENJ PASEK & JUSTIN PAUL

COME SUNDAY
from BLACK, BROWN & BEIGE

TROMBONE

By DUKE ELLINGTON

CRAZY

TROMBONE

Words and Music by
WILLIE NELSON

CRYING

TROMBONE

Words and Music by ROY ORBISON
and JOE MELSON

Moderately slow, with feeling

DREAM A LITTLE DREAM OF ME

TROMBONE

Words by GUS KAHN
Music by WILBUR SCHWANDT
and FABIAN ANDREE

DAUGHTERS

TROMBONE

Words and Music by
JOHN MAYER

CODA

D.S. al Coda

EASY LIVING
Theme from the Paramount Picture EASY LIVING

TROMBONE

Words and Music by LEO ROBIN
and RALPH RAINGER

ETERNAL FLAME

TROMBONE

Words and Music by BILLY STEINBERG,
TOM KELLY and SUSANNA HOFFS

ETERNALLY

TROMBONE

Words by GEOFFREY PARSONS
Music by CHARLES CHAPLIN

EVERY BREATH YOU TAKE

TROMBONE

Music and Lyrics by
STING

(EVERYTHING I DO) I DO IT FOR YOU

from the Motion Picture ROBIN HOOD: PRINCE OF THIEVES

TROMBONE

Written by MICHAEL KAMEN

FEELING GOOD

from THE ROAR OF THE GREASEPAINT – THE SMELL OF THE CROWD

TROMBONE

Words and Music by LESLIE BRICUSSE
and ANTHONY NEWLEY

FOR ALL WE KNOW

TROMBONE

Words by SAM M. LEWIS
Music by J. FRED COOTS

GABRIEL'S OBOE

from the Motion Picture THE MISSION

TROMBONE

Words and Music by
ENNIO MORRICONE

Slowly, expressively

GOOD NIGHT

TROMBONE

Words and Music by JOHN LENNON
and PAUL McCARTNEY

GOODNIGHT, SWEETHEART, GOODNIGHT
(Goodnight, It's Time to Go)

TROMBONE

Words and Music by JAMES HUDSON
and CALVIN CARTER

Moderately

HAVE I TOLD YOU LATELY

TROMBONE

Words and Music by
VAN MORRISON

HELLO

TROMBONE

Words and Music by
LIONEL RICHIE

HEAL THE WORLD

TROMBONE

Words and Music by
MICHAEL JACKSON

(small notes optional)

D.S. al Coda

CODA

HERE, THERE AND EVERYWHERE

TROMBONE

Words and Music by JOHN LENNON
and PAUL McCARTNEY

HIGHLAND CATHEDRAL

TROMBONE

By MICHAEL KORB
and ULRICH ROEVER

Stately March, in 2

I HAVE A DREAM

from MAMMA MIA!

TROMBONE

Words and Music by BENNY ANDERSSON
and BJÖRN ULVAEUS

D.S. al Coda

CODA

I LEFT MY HEART IN SAN FRANCISCO

TROMBONE

Words by DOUGLASS CROSS
Music by GEORGE CORY

I WILL

TROMBONE

Words and Music by JOHN LENNON
and PAUL McCARTNEY

I'LL BE AROUND

TROMBONE

Words and Music by
ALEC WILDER

Slowly, with expression

I'LL BE SEEING YOU

from RIGHT THIS WAY

TROMBONE

Written by IRVING KAHAL
and SAMMY FAIN

I'VE DREAMED OF YOU

TROMBONE

Words and Music by ANN HAMPTON CALLAWAY
and ROLF LOVLAND

IN MY ROOM

TROMBONE

Words and Music by BRIAN WILSON
and GARY USHER

LA VIE EN ROSE
(Take Me to Your Heart Again)

TROMBONE

Original French Lyrics by EDITH PIAF
Music by LUIGUY
English Lyrics by MACK DAVID

Slowly, with expression

JUST GIVE ME A REASON

TROMBONE

Words and Music by ALECIA MOORE,
JEFF BHASKER and NATE RUESS

LADY IN RED

TROMBONE

Words and Music by
CHRIS DeBURGH

Moderately slow

LET IT BE ME
(Je t'appartiens)

TROMBONE

English Words by MANN CURTIS
French Words by PIERRE DeLANOE
Music by GILBERT BECAUD

Moderately

LOST IN YOUR EYES

TROMBONE

Words and Music by
DEBORAH GIBSON

LOVE ME TENDER

TROMBONE

Words and Music by ELVIS PRESLEY
and VERA MATSON

LOVING YOU

TROMBONE

Words and Music by JERRY LEIBER
and MIKE STOLLER

Slowly, with a beat

LULLABYE
(Goodnight, My Angel)

TROMBONE

Words and Music by
BILLY JOEL

MIA & SEBASTIAN'S THEME

from LA LA LAND

TROMBONE

Music by
JUSTIN HURWITZ

MICHELLE

TROMBONE

Words and Music by JOHN LENNON
and PAUL McCARTNEY

MONA LISA

from the Paramount Picture CAPTAIN CAREY, U.S.A.

TROMBONE

Words and Music by JAY LIVINGSTON
and RAY EVANS

MY FOOLISH HEART

TROMBONE

Words by NED WASHINGTON
Music by VICTOR YOUNG

Slowly and expressively

MY FUNNY VALENTINE

from BABES IN ARMS

TROMBONE

Words by LORENZ HART
Music by RICHARD RODGERS

MY VALENTINE

TROMBONE

Words and Music by
PAUL McCARTNEY

MY WAY

TROMBONE

English Words by PAUL ANKA
Original French Words by GILLES THIBAULT
Music by JACQUES REVAUX and CLAUDE FRANCOIS

NANCY WITH THE LAUGHING FACE

TROMBONE

Words by PHIL SILVERS
Music by JAMES VAN HEUSEN

NATURE BOY

TROMBONE

Words and Music by
EDEN AHBEZ

NEVER ENOUGH

from THE GREATEST SHOWMAN

TROMBONE

Words and Music by BENJ PASEK
and JUSTIN PAUL

A NIGHTINGALE SANG IN BERKELEY SQUARE

TROMBONE

Lyric by ERIC MASCHWITZ
Music by MANNING SHERWIN

PERFECT

TROMBONE

Words and Music by
ED SHEERAN

PHOTOGRAPH

TROMBONE

Words and Music by ED SHEERAN,
JOHNNY McDAID, MARTIN PETER HARRINGTON
and TOM LEONARD

(small note optional)

THE PLACE WHERE LOST THINGS GO

from MARY POPPINS RETURNS

TROMBONE

Music by MARC SHAIMAN
Lyrics by SCOTT WITTMAN and MARC SHAIMAN

RAINY DAYS AND MONDAYS

TROMBONE

Lyrics by PAUL WILLIAMS
Music by ROGER NICHOLS

RELEASE ME

TROMBONE

Words and Music by ROBERT YOUNT,
EDDIE MILLER and DUB WILLIAMS

REWRITE THE STARS

from THE GREATEST SHOWMAN

TROMBONE

Words and Music by BENJ PASEK
and JUSTIN PAUL

SAILING

TROMBONE

Words and Music by
CHRISTOPHER CROSS

To Coda

D.S. al Coda

CODA

SCARBOROUGH FAIR/CANTICLE

TROMBONE

Arrangement and Original Counter Melody by
PAUL SIMON and ARTHUR GARFUNKEL

SHALLOW
from A STAR IS BORN

TROMBONE

Words and Music by STEFANI GERMANOTTA,
MARK RONSON, ANDREW WYATT
and ANTHONY ROSSOMANDO

SINCE I DON'T HAVE YOU

TROMBONE

Words and Music by JAMES BEAUMONT,
JANET VOGEL, JOSEPH VERSCHAREN,
WALTER LESTER, LENNIE MARTIN,
JOSEPH ROCK and JOHN TAYLOR

Slowly, with a strong, rockin' beat

SHE'S ALWAYS A WOMAN

TROMBONE

Words and Music by
BILLY JOEL

Quickly, in 1

SMILE
Theme from MODERN TIMES

TROMBONE

Words by JOHN TURNER and GEOFFREY PARSONS
Music by CHARLES CHAPLIN

Moderately, with great warmth

SMOKE GETS IN YOUR EYES

from ROBERTA

TROMBONE

Words by OTTO HARBACH
Music by JEROME KERN

SOMETHING WONDERFUL

from THE KING AND I

TROMBONE

Lyrics by OSCAR HAMMERSTEIN II
Music by RICHARD RODGERS

SOMEWHERE

from WEST SIDE STORY

TROMBONE

Lyrics by STEPHEN SONDHEIM
Music by LEONARD BERNSTEIN

THE SOUND OF SILENCE

TROMBONE

Words and Music by
PAUL SIMON

STARDUST

TROMBONE

Words by MITCHELL PARISH
Music by HOAGY CARMICHAEL

STRANGERS IN THE NIGHT

adapted from A MAN COULD GET KILLED

TROMBONE

Words by CHARLES SINGLETON
and EDDIE SNYDER
Music by BERT KAEMPFERT

SWAY
(Quien será)

TROMBONE

English Words by NORMAN GIMBEL
Spanish Words and Music by PABLO BELTRÁN RUIZ
and LUIS DEMETRIO TRACONIS MOLINA

TENNESSEE WALTZ

TROMBONE

Words and Music by REDD STEWART
and PEE WEE KING

Easy Waltz

(THERE IS) NO GREATER LOVE

TROMBONE

Words by MARTY SYMES
Music by ISHAM JONES

THEY SAY IT'S WONDERFUL

from the Stage Production ANNIE GET YOUR GUN

TROMBONE

Words and Music by
IRVING BERLIN

THREE TIMES A LADY

TROMBONE

Words and Music by
LIONEL RICHIE

TIME TO SAY GOODBYE

TROMBONE

Words by LUCIO QUARANTOTTO
and FRANK PETERSON
Music by FRANCESCO SARTORI

(small notes optional)

TRUE COLORS

TROMBONE

Words and Music by BILLY STEINBERG
and TOM KELLY

TRULY

TROMBONE

Words and Music by
LIONEL RICHIE

Slowly

UNEXPECTED SONG
from SONG & DANCE

TROMBONE

Music by ANDREW LLOYD WEBBER
Lyrics by DON BLACK

WE'VE ONLY JUST BEGUN

TROMBONE

Words and Music by ROGER NICHOLS
and PAUL WILLIAMS

WE'VE GOT TONIGHT

TROMBONE

Words and Music by
BOB SEGER

WHAT A WONDERFUL WORLD

TROMBONE

Words and Music by GEORGE DAVID WEISS
and BOB THIELE

WONDERFUL TONIGHT

TROMBONE

Words and Music by
ERIC CLAPTON

YESTER-ME, YESTER-YOU, YESTERDAY

TROMBONE

Words by RON MILLER
Music by BRYAN WELLS

YESTERDAY ONCE MORE

TROMBONE

Words and Music by JOHN BETTIS
and RICHARD CARPENTER

YESTERDAY, WHEN I WAS YOUNG
(Hier Encore)

TROMBONE

English Lyric by HERBERT KRETZMER
Original French Text and Music by CHARLES AZNAVOUR

YOU ARE THE SUNSHINE OF MY LIFE

TROMBONE

Words and Music by
STEVIE WONDER

YOU'RE THE INSPIRATION

TROMBONE

Words and Music by PETER CETERA
and DAVID FOSTER

YOUNG AT HEART

from YOUNG AT HEART

TROMBONE

Words by CAROLYN LEIGH
Music by JOHNNY RICHARDS

YOUR SONG

TROMBONE

Words and Music by ELTON JOHN
and BERNIE TAUPIN